HERstory

Lisa Marie's Wedding Diary

Shamelessly concocted
by Sean Kelly and Chris Kelly
Illustrated and designed by Ron Barrett

A John Boswell Associates Book

Villard New York

PERSONAL PRIVATE
DIARY OF

Lisa Marie Presley ~~Keough~~
~~Presley Jackson~~
(Presley)

NO SNOOPING!

THIS MEANS <u>YOU</u> MAMA!

AND <u>YOU</u> TO DANNY!

I really mean it!

Jan 1

Dear Diary Happy New Years

1994! NOT!!! I AM SO

BOREO!!!

My resolutions
1. Like Mama says stop making so many lists.
2. Get my act together.
3. Keep a diary every single day.

Feb 20
Dear Diary
guess what? I'm
ENGAGED!!! Boy
if my Daddy were
really dead he would be

turning over in his grave! Because
you'll never guess to who! Who to?
Whatever. Well anyways remember
that TV cartoon show I used to
watch when I was a kid right after

♥ ————

Eva ♡

from my scrap book ←

Scoobydoo about the 6 Mowtown-singing colored boys? Well my fiancee-to-be is none other than the one who was the cute little one! When I got home from my auditing session this aft (two big wins!) Mama told me "his people"

♥

had just now "popped the question" to "our people" by fax. I am so PSYCHED! Note to self – remember to tell Danny & the kids ASAP! I just hope Danny doesn't go all hissy & "hubby" on me. Well if he does he can <u>EAT</u> <u>IT!</u>

"FOREVER"

Feb 24

Dear Diary silly me how was I supposed to know that "my" Michael Jackson was the same Michael Jackson as THE Michael Jackson! You know the singer on "Beat It" & "Thriller" & etc.! Jeez

"Ben" was even "our song" for Danny & I! I always thought he was engaged to Brook whatsername -- you know the model who looks like Daddy used to (except he plucked his eyebrows)! Anyways today I went out & got a bunch of "Bride" magazines to look for a wedding dress. Danny & the kids think definitely "white" but Mama says maybe not.

Too tacky?

Inflatable mutton chop sleeves, white-on-white camo-silk, and a wide-load rear rose rise from a puddle of ivory tule to make "I do" a fashion statement.

Mar 1

Dear Diary well today was the BIG DAY I finally met M.J. himself in person at last & I take it back what I said about Daddy in his grave. Like Mama says E. didnt have a racial bone in his body & always said it doesnt matter what color you are green or polka dot or whatever as long as you dont **look** like an N Word which Michael definitely does NOT! And his voice even sounds like my role model Jackie O.! He was a perfect gentleman I mean he didnt " put the make " on me or anything. I flew out to Vegas for our first " date " & when I got there it was supposed to be a secret but reporters & photographers

♥ ————

were everywhere
bugging him
about just giving
a generous gift to
some little kid! If
you ask me the
so-called "media"
can EGT IT!

Mar 7
Dear Diary its
all set! Before to
long I will be
walking down the
isle!

Lisa M. Jackson

Mrs. Michael Presley

Mrs Michael Presley Jackson Jackson

Mrs. Michael Jackson

Mrs. Michael Jackson

Lisa Marie Presley Keough Jackson

Lisa Marie Presley Keough Jackson

Lisa M. Jackson

Mrs. M. Jackson   Mrs M. Jackson

Lisa Marie Presley Jackson

Mrs Michael Presley Jackson

The Queen of Pop

♥

Mar 10

Dear Diary last night I had a dream Mikey & I were married & had a baby. Possible names

    1. Lisa Marie Presley-Jackson Jr.

    2. L. Ron Presley-Jackson.

    3. **Not** Little Elvis for obvious reasons.

So today on the phone I asked my fiancee-to-be if he wants children & he said he'd been over all that with the District Attorney whatever that means.

♥

my
sweet

his
sweet

The Trump Tower—A New York Landmark

Mar 16
Dear Diary here I am in NY NYC
city staying at a hotel called the
Trump Tower! Mikey-poo invited me

up here to get to know his best friend Donald. Knowing Michael I expected to meet a duck! But **this** Donald owns the place! He is a fat rich sulky incredibly conceited white guy with long greasy hair. I like him. He kinda reminds me of Daddy. In fact this big hotel sweet (12 rooms!) where I'm staying even reminds me alot of Graceland. Only tacky.

Mar 19
Dear Diary you have no idea what a Big Star my fiancee-to-be is! Tonite I met him here in the hotel bar for a drink but Mikey is a Jehova Witless so he doesnt drink

♥

even beer so I said ask for a Shirley Temple & he did & 1/2 an hour later she **arrived** in person! P.S. She is **tons** older than she looks in her movies.

Apr 6
Dear Diary nothing new I am SO bored! M.J. & me & a bunch of his little rugrat pals spent the day in this big toy store right across the street. He was wearing like a doctors mask quote so no one will reckonize him. As IF. Wedding plans on hold. On the phone tonight Mama reminded me its one thing to hook a fish & another thing to real him in & how Daddy used to say quote a man dont buy a cow if he's getting his milk

♥

through the
fence. But I told
her that this here
Jackson fish doesnt
seem to want any
"milk" through the
fence or otherwise. Today the TV
news is all about a famous rock
singer Kurt Korbane or something
who just died. I cried because it
reminded me of Daddy. So many
famous rich great rock
stars die young! All
the more reason to get
this WEDDING
SHOW ON THE
ROAD!

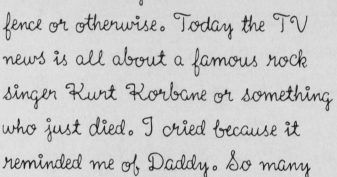

♥

April 9

Dear Diary its great to be back home
in LA! Reasons New York SUCKS
    1. Boring.
    2. Nothing to do.
    3. No malls.

April 13

Dear Diary Mama is SO SMART!
Today she said quote Buttonhead you
cant expect the man to marry you when
your already married. So I talked to
Danny & the kids & there cool so

♥

tomorrow I'm going to announce I'm getting a "dee eye vee oh are cee ee" & put the ball in his court.

April 16
Dear Diary
Mama says the best place to get a divorce is in the Dominican Republican which is the country where Grandpa

DEE

Vernon went to get rid of that bitch Dee because its foreign & sort of doesnt count if you want to take it back later. So thats ok.

♥

May 7

Dear Diary here I am at a beach in the Dominican Republican with Danny. Yesterday we got our No Sweat Divorce from some foreign geek but I must say last night when we came back to the hotel here it was like a second honeymoon for Danny & I if you know what I mean.

Danny
2 sweet
2 B
4 got
———
10

✳ ✳ ✳ ✳
4 big ones!

♥

May 19

Dear Diary

tonite on the TV news my role model
Jackie O. passed away. She was
beautiful & incredibly rich & nobody
minded her marrying that even more
incredibly rich older guy even if he
was a wierdo & a creep & if they did
mind as far as she was concerned they
could EAT IT! May her Force Be
With Me when M.J. & I start
negotiating the so-called "pre-nup"
tomorrow.

♥

May 20

Dear Diary here we are in Palm
Spring FlG at a mansion Mary
Leggo that belongs to Mikes pal
"the" Donald. Its alot like
Graceland only tacky but it does have
a beach. Last night on Mamas advice
I took a shot at "seducing" my
fiancee-to-be. After supper we were
sitting there on this
big bed in the dark
watching ET for like
the 100th time & I
pushed one of the
rugrats off of his lap
& snuggled up & stuck
my tounge in his ear.

Mar-a-Lago Club

"A real classy joint."

♥

Diary you wont believe this but
from the taste he had Revlon Blusher
INSIDE HIS EAR! So that was
THAT.

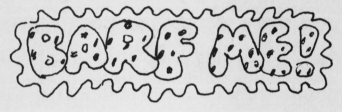

May 25
Dear Diary well tomorrow is MY
WEDDING DAY! What a drag
that after all my hopes & dreams &
all those practice Barbie Big Church
Weddings & singing "Go-IN to the
Chap-PEL of LOVE" this has to
be another hurry-up tacky little
service & I'm not even knocked up
this time! I about 1/2 expected
Daddy might show up to give his

♥

little girl away but I see in the Enquirer that he's hanging around that shopping mall in Kansas City again.

Guy who married us.

YABBA-DABBA-DOO!

MJ   LMP?

May 26
Dear Diary here I am an old married lady staying at Oscar Dulla Runta's (sp?) huge farm here in the Dominican Republican.

Its alot like Graceland only tacky.
For some reason or other MY
wedding service today was even
groddier than I imagined. It was in
this dinky little office & all in French
or Latin or something & my
"groom" kept giggling. I was so
pissed off that when I kissed him I
smeared his lipstick on purpose. Then
we came here. I have my own little
house & a huge TV but no cable.
Bummer. In my suitcase
when I unpacked I found
the sweetest note from
Mama about the wedding
night & how men are
animals & I'm a woman
now & etc. Actually my blushing

my foot

♥

groom is staying somewhere else getting his Beauty Sleep. But he says tomorrow the "romantic" honeymoon starts. We're going to Disney World.

May 30
Dear Diary
Disney World is just like Disney Land, only tacky.

Michael Mouse

June 1
Dear Diary living with someone is SO unromantic even if your not doing "it". This morning when I woke up I walked into the little girls room & caught Michael picking his

♥

nose. He finely chose the little pointy one. Anyways he says tomorrow we're flying to Europe. It would probably be tons cheaper to drive but hay its his money!

Cool Nails!

Love Poems
by Me

What is love?
Something from above?
A star, a moon
a balloon
who knows
what is love?

Happy thoughts of him
standing tall and slim
His big smile and eyes
Not like the other guys
I hope we never break-up
and I wish he wouldn't
use my make-up

How I found my lipstick
all messed up ———>

June 5

Dear Diary here in
Australia Europe we had
our first fight. I picked
up the phone in our hotel
sweet to call Mama & by
accident listened to Mike
on the extension for about 2 hours
wining & crying to his Best Friend
none other than Miss Elizabeth
Taylor the famous former movie star
& total INFLATO-SLUT who I
think of as the Purple Cow. He goes
she is SO understanding &
sympathetic to him. I go she better
keep her pudgy paws off of my
HUBBY.

Michaels
new German
pants

♥

June 7

Dear Diary heres how to tell if Liz Taylor the Purple Cow has been in your fridge

1. Even the open box of baking soda smells like "White Diamonds".

2. Fudge full of fingerprints of person who wears to many rings.

3. She drank up even the cooking Pepsi!

Whats the diff between a light bulb and Elizabeth Taylor from behind?

Light bulb

Elizabeth Taylor from behind

♥

June 16

Dear Diary Mike & I had another fight today about who has the right to hate Fathers Day more. I say me he says him.

Me Father wanders the earth pretending to be dead.

Him Father once towel-slapped Germane into a 3 week coma.

Me Father broke Mamas heart with Ann Margaret.

Him Father broke Mamas arm with tire iron.

Me Fathers likeness on shampoo bottles & back scratchers & snow domes.

Him Fathers likeness on every 2nd kid in Gary IND.

Me Father wanted a boy.

♥

Cool Shoes ♥

fun fur

"rocker"

loafer (get it?)

WONDER BREAD

flip fone

June 18

Dear Diary last night on TV I watched O.J. Simpson in his white Bronko & today guess who came over to the house? Only THE Johnny Cochrane who is O.J.s' lawyer & also M.J.s' lawyer! He was here telling Michael he should give even more money to some kids parents for some reason. So while "J.C." was here I asked him for the "inside scoop"

♥

about "O.J." He said quote my client is 100% innocent & your Daddy is alive & well & your husband is a sex machine with all the chicks.

July 3
Dear Diary today I got the sweetest fax from Linda who is the formerly cute Beatles wife. It said quote kid we are in the same boat. My advice is tell him that either you sing or you SING that is you want to get into the act or else you will call a press

conference & spill the beans about what a creep your married to. I showed it to M.J. & right away he asked me to co-star with him in a music video!

A Star is Born

July 12
Dear Diary I had an "early call" & we were "on the set" all day "shooting" the video for a song "You Are Not Alone".

♥

Here's a poloroid. Its supposed to be real sexy & all so both of us were actually NAKED for hours rolling around on this bed in front of the cameras under these lights which made me hot in more ways than one (get it?) Although he was careful that I never got a real look at his famous Spotted Thingy I actually thought we might end up doing "it". But at 6 oclock Michael said Cut & got up & put on my clothes & left.

♥

Aug 1

Today I officially announced our marraige to the so-called "media". It was even in all the papers. I said quote My name is Lisa Marie Presley-Jackson & etc. If they dont like it they can EAT IT.

Aug 7

Dear Diary here I am back in NYC NY New York in the Trump Tower again. I am so BORED while Michael spends every day & night in

the studio working on his new record.
He says he wants to call it "his
story". He says it will tell the true
story of his life. As IF!

Aug 8
Dear Diary I have
the most INCRED-
IBLE idea for
Mikey-poos "story
of his life" record!
What if he does ALL ELVIS
SONGS! (Guess who owns the
publishing?) Something like
Side 1
Poor Boy, Raised on Rock, In the
Ghetto, I'm Not the Marrying
Kind, Tutti Frutti, Young Dreams,

ELVIStory
by
Mikey-poo

Fairy Tale, Money Honey, Fame and Fortune, King of the Whole Wide World, Flaming Star, A House That Has Everything, Teddy Bear, Cotton Candy Land

Side 2

My Boy, My Little Friend, Little Darlin', Welcome To My World, Baby Let's Play House, Scratch My Back (Then I'll Scratch Yours), Dirty Dirty Feeling, Too Much Monkey Business, Suspicious Minds, I Got Stung, All My Trials, Jailhouse Rock

← my arm (drawn from life)

Aug 10

Dear Diary spent the day in the
control booth at the Hit Factory
listening to Mike sing his new song
called "They Don't Care About Us".
Its so totally great I got inspired &
wrote down some more "lyrics" he
could use

Kid me, yid me, under-bid me, Hose
me, oppose me, nickle nose me,

Double-biller me, Barry Diller me, Christ killer me, Spy on me, testify on me, Protocols of the Elders of Zion me, Old meany me, scaloppini me, gaberdine-stroking sheeny me, Oversee me, fricasee me, international Jewish Banking Conspiracy me & etc.

Aug 14

Dear Diary here I am in Hungery Europe. For once we didnt bring any of Mikes little rugrats who he calls his "Rubbas" with us. Instead we brought this midget Michu the Midget I guess so Mikeypoo can have someone who looks up to him. M.J. is going to do a video here

Michu

♥

where its cheap because the Hungerians
who he calls "real honkies"
used to be all Commies. He
spends all his time watching
some old boring black & white
Hitler movie over & over again
& taking notes & giggling. PS
Hungerian pizza SUCKS!

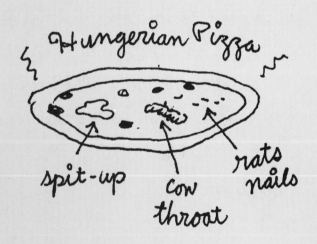

Hungerian Pizza

spit-up   cow   rats
           throat nails

Aug 17

Dear Diary tonight we had a "screening" of Mikes new video with the big statue of him in it. Its totally great but I heard some so-called "media" person say its like fashist. So I go what? & he goes like you know Mussolini. So I looked it up in a book.

4 ways Michael is not like Mussolini

1. Mussolini — Italian   Michael — Not Italian.

2. Mussolini — Scourge of Ethiopia   Michael — Often exchanges awards with Quincy Jones

♥

3. Mussolini - Il Duce Michael - Captain EO
4. Mussolini - Enemy of Tito Michael - Brother of Tito!

IL DUCE

IL DOUCHE

Aug 29

Dear Diary for Michaels Birthday Party today we went to Euro-Disney. It was totally great. We didnt have to line up for any of the rides. We had the place to ourselves there was nobody else there. I asked one of the tour guides if

Michael had made special arrangements but he said no its always like this.

Sept 4
Dear Diary here we are in Paris France. Today we went to see this place thats impossible to say or spell called Versailles which is alot like Graceland only tacky.

Souvenir de Versailles, France

Plus nobody speaks English. There are snotty foreigners everywhere!

Sept 8
Dear Diary tonight was the Grammy Awards Live on TV which began with me giving my beloved husband a great big kiss. We rehearsed everthing except the kiss itself I guess because M.J. was afraid I might get carried away with

♥

lust & accidently knock his new nose off or something. When we got our "cue" at the last minute he got scared & tried to back out but I told him to close his eyes & think of Gumby & it worked so well he FRENCHED me. Ug.

Sept 15
Dear Diary Mama says remember I'm a Southern Girl & I have gotta get started on the wedding present "Thank You" notes even though I hate almost all of them & wish I could tell them to EAT IT! Dear Brooke Shields & Diana Ross thank you so much for your autographed pictures they make great DART

♥

BOARDS. Dear Mr. Trump thanks so much for the thoughtful gift of your autographed book. How did you know we were out of kindling? Dear Mr. Speilberg thanks alot for the stuffed original ET he perfectly matches the Elephant Man bones in our den & etc.

Oct 3

Dear Diary today Mike came in while I was listening to a Madonna CD & he went totally batshit jealous calling her a dumb cow & a no talent ho & etc. 4 ways Michael & Madonna are different

　　1. Madonna nude pictures everywhere you look.

♥

Michael--cops taking pictures of his thingy quote horrible horrible experience.

2. Madonna dies her hair.
   Michael original hair color.

3. Madonna -- "Boytoy".
   Michael -- Settled out of court.

4. Madonna --Only "like" a virgin.

poss. "new looks"?

♥

Oct 16

Dear Diary at Neverland today I got
the wierdest phone call. It sounded
like a very very old old man & kind of
Italian. At first I thought O No!
Its that Mussolini guy & he's mad
about the video with the big statue.
But it turned out it was only Mr.
Frank Sinatra who I remember way
back my Daddy used to say was real
old even then. Anyways he was calling
because he wants to do a singing duet
with Mike. I said ok but not that
song about having things under your
skin. On the one about ordering out
for clowns. He got mad or something
& said quote Do you know who I

♥

am? So I said quote Go ask a nurse. So he goes if I was his daughter he'd pay to have me spanked. So I go if I was his daughter I'd wait till I got real old & then show everybody my ass in Playboy. Then he didnt say anything for a while & I realized he was asleep.

A JOKE

Q: Whats green and sings?

DOO
BEE
DOO
BEE
DOO

A: Frank SNOT-TRA!

get it?

♥

November 1

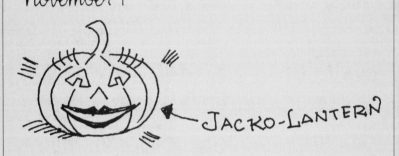

JACK-O-LANTERN

Dear Diary last night was Halloween.
M.J.s disguise was he went out trick
or treating door to door without any
make up on & scared all the neighbors
shitless.

November 21
Dear Diary we just had our quote
Family Thanksgiving Dinner at
Neverland. I went by helicopter & it
took forever there was so much smog. I
said quote I thought we'd never land.
But the pilot didnt get it. All night I

♥

kept losing count but I think all the Jacksons except Toyota were here chowing down only for some reason Mike was never in the same room as his sister Janet. Like he'd go out & a minute later she'd come in & visey versa. What gives?

Nov 22
Dear Diary for future reference heres 3 ways to get in trouble with Mikes Daddy Mr. Joe Jackson
1. Look quote cross eyed at Mr. Joe Jackson.
2. Quote sass-back Mr. Joe Jackson.
3. Call LaToya's 900 # then give him the phone say its for him.

♥

Nov 24

Dear Diary Neverland is a great place to visit if your a lama. It SUCKS! But Mike says whats the diff. between Graceland & Neverland?

1. Graceland -- Jungle Room.
   Neverland -- Jungle Gym.

2. Graceland -- Mystery Train.
   Neverland -- Mr. Toads Wild Ride.

3. Graceland -- Sonny & Red.
   Neverland -- Lamas.

4. Graceland -- "1 for the money, 2 for the show".
   Neverland -- Kids ride free.

6. Graceland -- Built by a white man who sounded like a black man.
   Neverland -- Built by Michael.

Also guys like Sonny & Red are great

♥

to have hanging around they always tell you you look terrific no matter how fat you get but with Guatamalan housemaids who dont speak English you cant even tell if there sucking up.

Dec 1
Dear Diary still at Michaels place Neverland.
Today I went with him & some of his special rugrat friends to tour his famous zoo. One kid asked him wheres Bubbles the Chimp? Mike said Bubbles isnt here anymore because he volunteered to go & do some important Ebola research.

♥

Dec 2

Dear Diary

you know how in hotels theres a Bible to read in every room?

Well here at Neverland theres this book about M.J.s hero Peter Pan I guess the "novelization" of the Disney movie. So last night I tried to read it although its in old English like Shakesbeer (sp?) or something.

Differences between M.J. & P.P.

1. P.P. goes into Wendy's bedroom. M.J. would never go in a girls bedroom.

2. P.P. hangs around with Fairies. M.J. hangs around with Barry Diller & David Geffin.

♥

3. P.P. doesn't wear lipstick.

Dec 3
Dear Diary today just "snooping"
around I found M.J.s Xmas list.
Talk about heartbreaking.

Ricky $150,000
Joshie $150,000
Jason $150,000
Asher $175,000
Dylan $150,000
Mac $150,000
Liza Marie — Hot
              wheels

♥

I couldnt stand it so I moved back here to my house in Hidden Hills CA & believe me theres no place like home.

Dec 4
Dear Diary yesterday when we were Xmas shopping on Rodeo Mama reminded me that for financial purposes a wedding isnt legal unless its been concentrated which means we have to do it at least once. Yuk! I

told her No Way. I said my husbands idea of monkey business is buying & selling monkeys. She goes well maybe he's buy sexual. I go well for sure nobody would give it to him for free!

Dec 19
Dear Diary today on the phone Mike was trying to get out of coming here to Hidden Hills for Xmas which he says he hates especially Santa Claus. I felt like teasing him so I said quote I would of thought you'd like the idea of a wierdly dressed grownup trying to buy affection from kids by giving them expensive gifts. But he didnt get it. He

♥

said no its that
sad song about
the rain deer with
the nose everyone
makes fun of.

Dec 20
Dear Diary I'm so upset about how
its going to be a "Blue Xmas" like
Daddy used to say! Today I was
telling Mama about my most
treasure memory of being
a little girl at Graceland
this time of year sitting
around just like a real
family & watching Daddy
put a bullet through a

Charlie Brown Xmas. We both had a
good cry remembering & then she said
she'd call her Son In Law & use her
Southern wiles on him & quote tell
that little prick to get with the
program.

Dec 22
Dear Diary well its all set Mike is
coming here for Xmas & so is Mama
only she says she'll leave us 2
love birds alone & it
will be our chance
to concentrate the
marraige. It's
so gross she's

UG!

giving me hints on quote seducing him.
Sexy lingerie she says like Victorias
Secret. I said that wont work but if I
get desperate I might try something by
Oshkosh.

Dec 25
Dear Diary Merry
Christmas. As IF! Last
night we had some wine
(I told M.J. it was
grape Hi C) & a fire
in the fireplace &
Mama kept hinting around
about you 2 love birds. Gag me!
Anyways Michael did sleep over & in
the middle of the night I was half
asleep & I thought maybe he was

♥

finely trying something but it turned
out I'd just rolled over on the Itty
Bitty Book Lite.

Dec 26
Dear Diary well
at least I found
out why M.J. is
so freaked out about
Xmas. Today before
he went home he
started telling me
about his childhood
memories of Xmas back in Gary Ind
like how his father Mr. Joe Jackson
used to hang his little stocking by the
fireplace while he was still wearing it
& etc. Although I think the part about

♥

once seeing Mr. Joe Jackson strangle
an elf was just a dream.

❧❧❧❧❧❧❧❧❧❧❧❧❧❧❧

Jan 1
Dear Diary Happy New Years 1996!
NOT!! Mamas always saying Mike
is quote just like your Daddy! So I
made a list of how there SO alike.
NOT.

   1. Daddy was my POP & the
   KING. Michael is only the King
   of Pop.
   2. Daddy couldn't show his hips
   on Ed Sullivan. Michael sounds
   like Topo Gigio.
   3. Daddy told the FBI he'd dig up

♥

info to destroy the Beatles. Michael sold "Revolution" to a Korean sneaker Co.

Jan 3

Dear Diary Mama says quote Buttonhead your so negative. If your going to make lists make a list of the **GOOD** things about living with your husband So ok.

1. He never leaves the toilet seat up.

♥

Feb 1

Dear Diary today was my Birthday.
Only 3 X 356 days before Daddys
estate is mine all M I N E & I can
tell whoever I want to <u>EAT</u> <u>IT!</u>
Met Danny for a b.d. lunch. It
brought back fond memorys &
reminded me of a Heraldo show I saw
quote Help I'm falling in love with
my former ex-mate! Tonite my
so-called Birthday Party was with
M.J. & some over the hill Mowtown

♥ ————

"stars" & little white rugrats at his favorite Chinese restaurant. God I could strangle him everytime he orders quote One Young Hung Gay Guy & "Miss" Ross giggles like its this big witty "inside" joke. As IF. But the most INCREDIBLE thing that happened was my fortune cookie. This is it.

For God's sake, get out!

Diary as you know I'm not in the least bit superstitious but I thing that means something.

♥

Feb 25

Dear Diary I am so bored I think I should write a book. The story of my life. I bet it would sell like a bitch. But should it be a biography or something classier? An autobiography? Anyways I have a GREGT title for it.

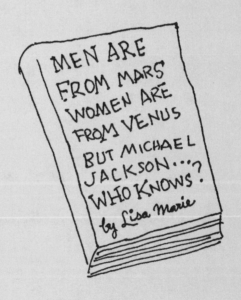

MEN ARE FROM MARS WOMEN ARE FROM VENUS BUT MICHAEL JACKSON...? WHO KNOWS? by Lisa Marie

♥

Feb 27

Dear Diary today was Elizabeth the Purple Cow's birthday (#100?) but M.J. couldnt go out in public to her big party because at the moment he is "between noses" so he spent the whole day watching his entire collection of her stupid movies on video. My "favorites" are

Who's Afraid of Virginia Wolf – Fatty fat fat! She gets the strangling she deserves plus her hair needs conditioning!

X Y and Zee – Must weigh a ton! Plus gets slapped!

Under Milk Wood – Slapped around plenty!

♥

Reflections in a Golden Eye – Lard butt on view plus slapping galore! The Sea Wife – Its actually Joan Collins in it with Richard Burton but it would make Liz crazy to know I thought it was her!

March 10
Dear Diary to celebrate finishing his stupid HISstory record guess who my so-called "husband" invited to lunch? The Purple Cow!!! While he was out of the room she told me she was sure I would be just as happy with M.J. as

♥

she had been with Malcome Forbes &
then she laughed so hard she spit up a
lamb chop.

Rules to remember when lunching
with Liz

    1. Forks & spoons are for sissies.

    2. Me casserole es su casserole.

    3. Meatballs that fall on the
carpet are still " in play."

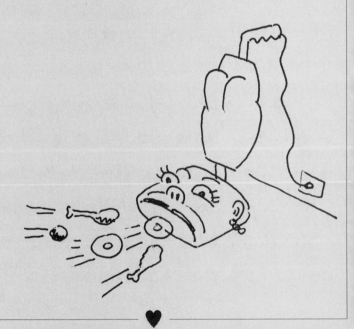

♥

Apr 1

Dear Diary Happy April Fools Day!
I thought of the perfect prank on the
Purple Cow I phoned a pizza place &
told them NOT to deliver a dozen pies
to her place. But my husband has no
sense of humor! Here are just 3 of my
practicle jokes he didn't enjoy today

♥

1. "snapping" the elastic on his surgical mask.
2. short-sheeting the oxygen chamber.
3. the old "I've got your nose" trick.

April 21
Dear Diary the creepiest things about Easter at Neverland
1. Mr. Joe Jackson comes for family dinner & strangles a rabbit.
2. Michaels Easter bonnet collection.
3. The neighborhood kids come for an Easter egg hunt & all the eggs "just happen" to be hidden in Michaels pockets.

♥

May 3

Dear Diary this guy SONY keeps calling here at my house looking for Michael screaming about wheres the rest of the new record its late & there going to sue & etc. I thought Chinese people were suppose to be so polite. So to shut him up I told him Michaels been busy doing alot of PBS TV for kids dressed like a purple dinasoar.

May 26

Dear Diary today was our 1st anniversary which my so-called "husband" completely forgot but his mother

didnt. She got me on the phone & said I sounded disappointed but she said quote all marraiges are disappointing honey child & she said

my eye (sketch from life)

sometimes Mr. Joe Jackson took her for granted & sometimes even when he was strangling her she suspected he was thinking of some other woman. She said she wondered if she'd be hearing the pitterpatter of little feet around her sons house soon & I said you dont ever hear much else around there. Except sometimes giggles and shrieks.

← a tear fell here

♥

June 1

Dear Diary tomorrow to promote his
stupid record M.J. & I have to do a
TV interview with Diane Sawyer who
I have always thought of as That
Stuckup Bitch so we have spent the
day rehearsing. Captain Eee-Yuck is
practicing his expression of shock
about the scheduled suprise buttlicking
phone- in call from the Purple Cow &
I am wrecking my brain trying to
find the perfect put-down come-back if
Miss Nosey gets to personal.

It takes one to know one.

Bite me.

When did Barbara Walters die and
leave you Queen?

Same to you.

♥

Nya nya nya nyanya.
As IF!
Mind your own beeswax.
Well DUH!
<u>EAT IT!</u>

Hawaiian man

June 16
Dear Diary here I
am in Hawai on a
well deserved vacation with Danny after
being grilled in the 3rd degree by Diane
"do you do it?" Sawyer on
TV. If she's so interested
in other peoples love life she
should of seen what went on
down on the beach last night
after the Hawian Loo-ow

♥

(sp?). This AM in the shower I found sand in places I didnt even know I had places. I must admit I'm starting to have 2nd thoughts about my wedding vows to M.J. which were actually in Spanish a language I got an F in by the way.

July 4
Dear Diary today was Independence Day so I told Mama I want a divorce. From Michael I mean. She went batshit about community

property & etc. & said Buttonhead
you need grounds like income
patability. So ok. Reasons he & I
are income patible

1. He is on the road alot
performing I am a stay-at-home
type.
2. I am a cat person he is a lama
person.
3. He thinks there is a jackpot when
you land on Free
Parking I say read
the rules stupid.
4. I think he might be
from outer space or
something.

Moon-
walk

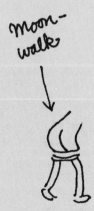

♥

July 10

Dear Diary Mama says if I divorce Michael I will end up an Old Maid but I said there are tons of eligible guys out there & started a list with PROs & CONs for instance

1. Hank Williams Junior

PRO. An all round dream boat who knows what its like to have a famous Daddy but not inherit one bit of talent.

CON. All his rowdy buddies.

2. Garth Brooks

PRO. A Star with a capital S.

CON. Capital LLPGIAH for Looks Like Phil Gram In A Hat.

3. M.C. Hammer

♥

PRO Does "it" with "women".
CON Might have been a "flash in the pan".

4. K.D. Lang

PRO. Charisma talent sex appeal fame $$$.

CON. He seems to be hiding something . . .

♥

July 20

Dear Diary more reasons M.J. & I are income patible

1. He eats all the cashews out of the mixed nuts.
2. He used my razor to shave the monkeys legs. Owzzie-wowzie!
3. I am more mature than he is & got over being Boy Crazy years ago.

Aug 2

Dear Diary on Mamas advice today I was at Neverland looking for "evidence" & I met one of the servants Miko Brando. He isnt Guatamalan at all in fact his Daddy is Marlon Brando the Godfather movie actor. We started talking about how it would be great to get his Daddy & my Daddy together again. But there are problems like my Daddy being scientifically dead & the government of French Polynesia not liking Mr. Brando moving around to much because it screws up the tides.

mB on Tahiti

Aug 3
Dear Diary I dont want to get parannoyed but this is something I found while I was sneaking around

Neverland looking for "evidence". I think its a report from private detectives M.J. hired to look for reporters weaknesses before he decided to do that Oprah interview.

CONFIDENTIAL

-Oprah : Smoked crack.
-Mike Wallace : Did not smoke crack.
-Oprah : Can't get Steadman to commit.
-Mike Wallace : Happily married to Andy Rooney. 1 child, Chris.
-Oprah : Crazy yo-yo dieting.
-Mike Wallace : Has maintained same weight since entering public life shortly after American Civil War.
-Oprah : Show has profiled gay marriages over 500 times.
-Mike Wallace : Show has profiled Vladimir Horowitz only 73 times.

♥

Sept 16
Dear Diary
well it hap-
pened finely in
the paper
today Dear
Annie answered
my letter!

Dear Annie: I and my husband who I will call "Peter" have been married for just over a year. "Peter" works very hard at his job and is very kind but he is not the man I expected. Our marriage has been one big disappointment after another. Not only did we not do "the act" on our honeymoon, but the only time we even "cuddle" is when he thinks people are watching. Also his family is strange. And he is always on the phone with an old girlfriend who I will call "Ava Gardner." I know there is nothing romantic between them because she is old and fat and usually drunk but still I get jealous. Also our house is full of guests and pets so we have no privacy. Annie if I did not have my Church and children and my other husband I would be so lonely. I would end this marriage right now but I do not want to be a laughing stock. Should I seek counseling?

NEEDY, IN NEVERLAND

Dear Needy: Count your blessings, kiddo, you could be married to that freak Michael Jackson.

Sept 29

Dear Diary at Neverland again looking for "evidence" today I ran into the parents of the latest rugrat who spent the weekend here. They came to pick up there kid & had to wait for hours. They said what goes on? I said your kids in his bedroom with a guy who wears lipstick & make up & likes to grab his crotch in public & scream I'm Bad I'm Bad! So what do YOU think GOES ON?

Oct 9

Dear Diary I think I may have found a legal loop hole out. I was looking at that crummy video some friend of M.J. took of our wedding & I swear to God you can tell right at the exact moment I said the Spanish for I do which is Si I'm trying to cross my fingers behind my back!

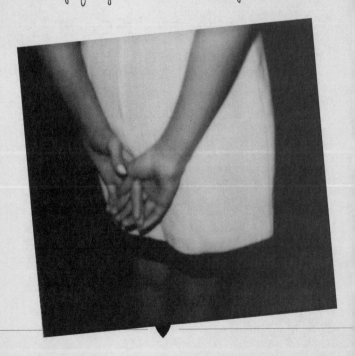

Mrs. Lisa Marie Presley Keough Jackson Keough

Nov 10

Dear Diary I was in such a good
mood this morning when I woke up &
Danny had started the coffee all by
himself & then I opened Variety &
thats how I found out MY
so-called " H U S B A N D " is going
to N Y in Dec. to do a concert for

♥

HBO. I guess they must be running out of Garey Bussey movies to show. I know its just to get out of spending another Xmas with me & Mama

Nov 20
Dear Diary
you know I
am " A "
political but if
anybody even a
world leader
has big hair &

Mr. Bill

a wide bottom & is a Good Old Southern bully boy the kind who reminds me of Daddy I cant help it I just dig him. Thats why if I voted I

♥

would of voted for Mr. Bill Clinton. (Also I feel sorry for him married to that stuck up blond bitch who reminds me of Diane Sawyer). But call me fickle because for the exact same reasons as above I am now just the Bigggest Fan of Mr. Bills #1 enemy Mr. Newt. Whenever I watch him on the C Span talking about Family Values & etc it gets me all hot and bothered. So anyways Diary I am so desperate that on impulse today I sat down & wrote my dream boat Mr. Newt a letter in Washington & asked for his statesmanlike advice.

U.S. House of Representatives
Office of the Speaker

Dear Mrs. Jackson-Presley,

Thank you for your kind letter of support for our legislative programs. I concur with your beautifully expressed sentiment that "the American Family is the basic building block of the backbone of the moral fibre of our society" but I also agree that sometimes divorce is a painful necessity, especially when financial considerations (or career aspirations) are involved.

In my experience the ideal place to "break the bad news" to one's spouse is a hospital.

With all personal best wishes,

Newt

p.s. Lisa Marie, next time you're in town, y'all drop by now, y' hear?

♥

Dec 1

Dear Diary today a letter came from Mr. Newt himself! I shall treasure it always!

Dec 8

Dear Diary yesterday I received the tragic news that my beloved Michael had collapsed on stage in NYC NY while rehearsing for his HBO cable show! My God when I heard he was struck down in his Prime Time I felt just like Yoko or even my role model Jackie O. & spent the whole day frantically shopping Rodeo for a black dress before rushing to his bedside here in NY. While here I took the opportunity tonite to follow Mr.

♥

Newts statemanlike advice. Of course
Mike was devastated. I'm sure I
saw a tear in his eye as he asked me to
please move because I was blocking
his view of the movie on TV. The
Disney channel natch. Peter Pan.

Feb 14
Dear Diary just
when my life was
getting back to
normal with
Mama Danny
& the kids
M.J. & his
team of evil lawyers have
halled me into court fighting for

My
DADDY
The
King

♥

custody of everything including Graceland Daddys catalog even the surviving Jordonaires! It is a Media Circus & the jury looks like its made up of all Jacksons giving me dirty looks. There are tears in there eyes as Johnny Cochrane is summing up in that unfair minority way of his preaching to them quote If the Underoos dont fit you must aquit!

And then I woke up. It was all just a horrible dream!

Thanks to:

Becky & Jessica Barrett, John Boswell, Patty Brown, Ward Calhoun, Beth Pearson, Dan Rembert, and David Rosenthal (who started it).

HERstory. Lisa Marie's Wedding Diary was totally made up, just for fun (and with all due respect to all members of the Jackson and Presley clans), by Sean and Chris Kelly, who are sometimes said to be among the top dozen or so Canadian-born, bicoastal, father-and-son comedy-writing teams. Chris, formerly an editor of _SPY_ and staff writer for the David Letterman show, has a fancy L.A. office as an associate producer of _Politically Incorrect with Bill Maher_. His old man, once a _National Lampoon_ editor and _Saturday Night Live_ staff writer, now works out of a drafty basement in Brooklyn. He is, nevertheless, the co-author (with Rosemary Rogers) of the books _Saints Preserve Us!_ and _Who In Hell..._ Ron Barrett, who drew all the pictures, is an illustrator and writer, and the artful forger of _O.J.'s Legal Pad_. Design and production were executed by Knickerbocker.

♥

♥